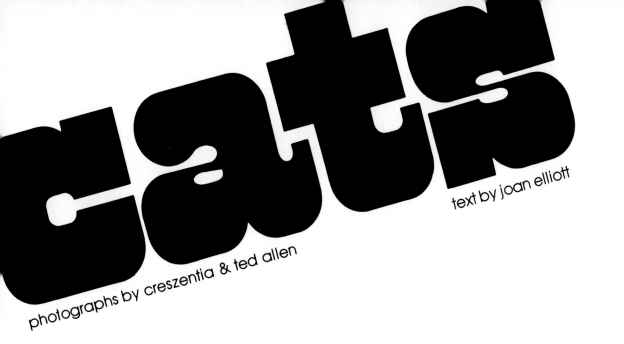

cats

photographs by creszentia & ted allen

text by joan elliott

a ridge press book | grosset & dunlap | new york

Library of Congress Catalog Card Number: 78-58093
ISBN: 0 — 448 — 16263 — 6
ISBN: 0 — 448 — 13484 — 5 (Library Edition)
Published simultaneously in Canada.
Printed and bound in the Netherlands.

cats

Though the cat is a familiar, everyday sight, he is one of the most remarkable creatures on earth. If you don't have a cat as a pet, you probably know someone who does. There are always neighborhood cats, resting on a stair, crouching under a car, lying in the sun. Everyone is used to cats and everyone has an opinion about them. When asked whether they like cats, few people will say they don't care. Some will say that they would rather have a dog; others will say that cats make them sneeze. And then there are people who talk affectionately about their cat for hours. Down the street there may be a lonely old man who has a houseful of cats to keep him company. But like them or not, no one can deny that cats are one of our closest and most uncommon companions.

Since the time cats first came into our homes, about 5,000 years ago, people have held strong ideas about them. In ancient Egypt, small wild cats were attracted to grain storehouses, where there were rats and mice for them to feed on. The Egyptians lured the cats into their homes, and they became friends. Later, Egyptians believed that cats had the power to heal the sick and control crops and livestock. There was even a cat goddess. Cats spread throughout the world and were favored by Greeks, Phoenicians, and Romans. But by the Middle Ages, people had changed their minds about cats. They now believed cats were evil and helped witches in their craft. Cats were feared, hunted, and tortured. This bad reputation lasted for many years, and even today there are traces — the unlucky black (or in Europe, white) cat, the Halloween cat. But now cats have safe places in homes all over the world.

No matter how much a pet the cat has become, a part of him is still the lone hunter in the wild that he was so long ago. Watch a cat outdoors. He is alert to every sound and movement. His muscles tense and in an instant he is ready to spring. His claws become dangerous weapons that can harm animals much bigger than himself. If a mouse or bird is nearby, he will silently stalk it, pounce on it, play with it, kill it, and proudly bring it to his owner, expecting praise for his good work. His speed, balance, ability to climb trees, jump high, and squeeze through small spaces make him a champion athlete. At night, his eyes take on a special glow that allows him to see better than most animals.

Cats—both big and small—can and do survive in the wild. But once a cat is at home indoors, it is hard to believe that this cuddly, purring creature is the same one that was outside. When you see a cat yawn, stretch, and curl up and go to sleep after his dinner, you know that he is quite contented and prefers the comforts of home. This is when a cat becomes more of a pet, living peacefully with his owner, and less of a wild animal. We know that outside a cat can take care of himself, but once inside he counts on people.

A cat is not a difficult pet to look after. He can entertain himself for hours, playing with the specks in the floor tiles or batting around a spool of thread he has discovered under the couch. He washes himself constantly and does not have to be told to go to bed. But no matter how independent a cat is said to be, he does need love, proper food, a warm home, and daily brushing. He should be watched closely to see that he is healthy, with regular visits to the vet.

Did you ever wonder why your cat sits directly in front of the television you're trying to watch, stands on the letter you're trying to write, or follows you around the house? It is because he needs you and your attention.

You will find that your cat has his own special personality. A timid cat will hide under the couch or in the bedroom when visitors arrive. But a bolder cat will come right up to investigate or even try to dash out the door. There are many ways your cat tells you things. A certain meow means "Please feed me," or "I'm watching some birds out the window and it's quite interesting," or "I want to be left alone right now." He uses different sounds to get his messages across. Besides the various kinds of meows, he can hiss, growl, scream, and wail. And of course, there is the purr, the sound of contentment and satisfaction.

We have come to depend on cats almost as much as they depend on us. If the owner sees that his cat is well cared for and happy, he will be rewarded with his pet's trust and affection.

Cats have coats that
come in all different colors,
lengths, and textures. This impish
kitten (left) is called a Rex,
and has a silky warm coat of
naturally curly hair. Even his whiskers
are wavy. He has one blue and
one copper eye, called odd-eyed.
Two big eyes are staring out of the
ball of fluff above. This kitten
is a Blue Persian, and his long and
soft coat has a bluish tone.

Preceding pages: This family of
Seal Point Siamese kittens is
holding still long enough for a
picture to be taken, but will soon
resume its antics. It's a hard job
to keep six playful kittens quiet
for even a few moments, but the
photographers' most important tools,
besides their cameras, are patience
and love for their subjects. They can
bring out the personality in any
breed of cat, pedigreed or not. The
Brown Tabby Shorthair (left) with the bright
pink tongue is alert and ready to explore.
The tabby markings are the dark bars
or stripes on its face and coat.
More reserved, the Chinchilla (below)
seems used to being photographed.

Many breeds of cats visit the Allens' studio to have their pictures taken. Some are nervous and must become used to the new surroundings, so they are soothed and cared for until they feel comfortable. The Red Persian and odd-eyed White Persian (upper left and right) are relaxed and even pose so the camera gets their best sides. A blue domestic (above) winks at the camera.

Blue Cream Persian (upper left) is not a
new kind of dessert but a rare breed. There
are very few males of its kind. Its coat
has color patches of blue and cream. Waiting
for its picture to be taken, this white domestic
(upper right) decided to take a quick catnap.
A Brown Tabby Persian (above) selected her
own background by curling up near
some driftwood in the studio.

Preceding pages: Georgia Girl (left), a
Blue Cream Persian, has the grandeur of her
relative the lion. This famous cat is a grand
champion in the U.S.A. One of the newest breeds
to the cat world is the Scottish Fold (right).
A cat with folded ears was discovered on a
farm in Scotland in 1961. This one, Kinsey,
has classic Brown Tabby markings. Above:
This Calico Persian has a coat patched in red,
cream, black, and white. It is also
called Tortoiseshell and White. Right: A
perfect wedge-shaped head and brilliant
blue eyes are some of the characteristics that
make this Blue Point Siamese a grand
champion. As Siamese owners know, these
cats have an unusual cry and like to "talk."

Kittens are natural comedians,
and the best way to take a
picture is to let the kittens do
the job. If they are carefully
chosen and cared for, kittens are
lively companions. Make sure
your kitten is two or three months old
before he is taken from the litter.
He should have bright eyes and a shiny
coat. You can comfort a new kitten
by talking to him, holding him gently,
and placing a soft blanket in his basket.

No room for more: This perky black and white cat (below) is comfortable in a one-cat bushel. Like soft balls of yarn, Tonkinese kittens (right) nestle in a sewing basket. A new and rare breed, the Tonkinese is a combination of Burmese and Siamese. For sleeping, kittens prefer warm baskets, but as they grow up, they find other places—the top of a radiator or tv, a comfortable chair, or just a particular corner of the carpet.

Timid Abyssinian kittens (above) peek over the rim of a copper dish, while a bolder one explores the handle. Abys are shy cats and are slow to make friends, but when they do, owners find them loyal and affectionate companions. A perfect present, this copper-eyed White Persian (left) is one of the most glamorous breeds.

Like two little cream puffs, these six-week-old Shaded Silver kittens (above) rest in an antique china dessert dish. An alluring odd-eyed White Persian (below) in a copper pot is appropriately named Glamour Boy. Show cats must be groomed often. To keep their coats clean, a shampoo and bath followed by a comb-out and blow-dry is often necessary.

Preceding pages: Golden eyes like saucers
and rich brown coat make the Burmese
Brown seem mysterious. The breed also comes
in such delicious colors as chocolate, cream,
and lilac. He is a popular house pet, and
has a voice like that of a Siamese, but softer.
  Tiffany special: The lucky mother of
these jeweled kittens had her litter of eleven
on the Allens' lawn. So the kittens
wouldn't freeze, they were taken inside. The
mother was encouraged to join her kittens,
but she was too wild. Soon all the kittens
had homes. The one above, too irresistible to
give away, was kept.

Preceding pages: If you watch carefully, a cat's face will always tell you what mood he is in. How would you guess the cat on the left is feeling right now? Twelve years ago the Allens rescued the cat on the right, who had run away from home, and named him Schnüle (it means "caress" in German). Since then, he has become one of the most photographed cats in the world, posing for magazines, books, and commercials. He is so calm and gentle that confusion, noise, and bright lights don't bother him.

Cats are famous for their curiosity. Your pet will explore his home and everything in it. Valuable, breakable objects should be put away or out of reach. Remember that cats are hunters and can jump and climb onto even the highest shelf.

Cats love to play—with toys, with other cats, with their owners, or just by themselves. When kittens play, they are getting experience for adult life, learning how to attack and defend themselves. But do not be alarmed if their play seems too rough—one will let the other know when he has had enough, and neither will be harmed. Though kittens keep busy and active, they tire easily and will soon want to take a nap. Your new kitten will want you to play—gently—with him, but remember to let him rest after about fifteen minutes. Kittens are delicate creatures and require lots of sleep. Following pages: Kittens of any breed— here a domestic red tabby—are appealing. Domestics are readily available for a small fee or free from an animal shelter or neighborhood litter.

Happy families: Mother cats are devoted
to their kittens and give them loving and
attentive care. After giving birth to
her litter, she cleans and licks her
kittens, feeds them and watches constantly
to make sure no harm comes to them or that
a curious kitten does not stray. Later,
she teaches them, plays with them,
and advises them — a complete education.
If she feels her nest is in danger, she
will defend it at all costs. One
mother carried each of her nine
endangered kittens almost a mile to
safety. If the father is present, he
will help the mother — if not, she will
often ask humans for help.

Fiercely protecting her kittens, a
mother Korat says by the look in
her eyes that it's all right to watch,
but just don't get too close. These
kittens will feed on their mother's
milk until they are about four weeks old.
Then, by imitating their mother, they
learn to lap milk from a saucer. This is
when the owner can help. Be sure to
ask the veterinarian exactly what to feed
the newborn kittens in your house.
They will need about five meals a day
until they are eight weeks old.
By this time, kittens are ready to
leave their mother. They finally become
cats when they are about a year old.

Above: Like a king in royal robes,
this cat seems to gaze down on his
subjects. This is the elegant Turkish
Angora, who really is from Turkey.
He has a slender body, silky, deep fur,
and a long fringed tail. People say
that when this cat lives in the country,
he loves to swim. His nickname is
Swimming Cat. Left: The ancient Egyptians
worshiped cats similar to this Abyssinian.
The Abby's coat looks like that of a rabbit's.
Right: This unusual cat is a Calico Rex.

Best friends: Cats and other animals
can get along well if they are brought
up together. Charlie the Squirrel fell
out of his nest and was saved by the
Allens, who had also just rescued a kitten
named Jungle Baby. When both animals
were being nursed back to health, they
became friends on a heating pad. The
beagle below is using Schnüle as a pillow.
If you introduce a new puppy to your
cat, watch them carefully to see that
they do not harm each other. When
they get used to the other's presence
they will probably become friends.

By the sea: Can the Seal Point
Siamese kittens below want to take
a swim? Most cats don't like the water,
but if one accidently falls in,
he can save himself by—believe it
or not—doing the dog paddle.
He is able to keep his head above
water until he gets to land.
Lynx Point kittens (right), posed on
driftwood, seem to be listening
to the roaring ocean behind them.

Country cats: Do you ever wonder where your cat goes when you let him out? If you've ever tried to follow him, you know that he can disappear in a flash. Outdoors he becomes more of a wild cat and less of a pet. He is always on the lookout for birds, rabbits, dogs. Notice how his ears follow every sound like radar, how swiftly he can pounce, how intently he watches the slightest movement. But, as you know, when he gets tired, cold, or hungry, he is soon meowing at your door.

Preceding pages: Playful kittens
will grow into dignified cats, such
as the Maine Coon Cat on the right.
This is probably the only breed that
originated in the United States. He
is quite large and has a heavy coat with
a ruff around his neck that protects
him from cold weather. Because
people once thought he was part
raccoon, they named him Coon Cat.
These picture-perfect cats (above and
left) will grace any household.

Preceding pages: The shape of this blue-eyed Persian (left) is lost in a white cloud of fur. His long coat needs brushing twice a day. An occasional bath is necessary, also, to keep his coat from yellowing. The shorthaired Brown Tabby (right) needs to be brushed only once a day. He won't need a bath unless he gets tar, gasoline, or other harmful substances on his coat. A cat keeps clean by licking himself, and anything he gets on his coat is soon in his mouth.

Schnüle (bottom right) bats around a plastic toy, and a Persian (below) adopts a lookalike friend.

Preceding pages: Cats' cradle —
These Persian kittens already have
the rich color of champion cats.
A Silver Tabby (top), a Manx
(above), and a Burmese (right), strike
stylish poses for the camera. Do you
notice anything missing from the Manx?
This one doesn't have a tail, though
some of this breed do. Manx cats without
tails are called "Rumpy"; those with
short tails are called "Stumpy."

In a garage, shivering in an old coat,
were ten orphan kittens. Someone had left
them to fend for themselves. Luckily,
they were found, fed, and cared for until
they became healthy. These two tabbies
(left) are purring with pleasure to be safe
and warm. Scientists still don't know
exactly how a cat purrs. If you put your
hand on a purring cat's throat, you can
feel the vibrations. Purring can be loud
or soft, depending on how happy a cat is.
Cats also purr when they are frightened.
Another way cats show pleasure is by
washing or grooming other cats or people.
If a cat licks your hand, you know
he is glad to have you there.

A ribbon, a spool of thread, a catnip
mouse may amuse a kitten for hours. But
an owner should always be careful when
choosing a pet's toy. Kittens like to chew
and may swallow small objects, though
adults are usually more careful. Though
kittens love to play with balls of yarn,
this should not be encouraged because they
may try to eat the yarn and choke.

Following pages: People wanted a
Siamese with long hair, so a new breed called
the Himalayan was created. Actually, this breed
has a Siamese's coloring and a Persian's body.
This Himalayan (left) is a Seal Point, but there
are also Blue, Chocolate, Flame, Lilac, and Tortie
points. The striking Burmese kittens (right)
in the copper kettle are Ariadne and Thais.

Brainy and beautiful. Are cats smart?
Some people think that because a cat doesn't
obey an owner's command, the pet doesn't
understand it. But when you give your cat
an order and he just stares back at you—or
maybe even does the opposite—you
know he understands but simply does not like
to be told what to do. We know cats are
beautiful. These champion Shaded Silvers
(opposite) are just back from the show.
     Following page: Precious treasures—
Egyptian Maus have coats of Silver or Gold.